SLOW COOKER RECIPE BOOK
FOR 2 PEOPLES

TABLE OF CONTENTS

I. INTRODUCTION

What is Slow ... 1
Why Use a Slo... ...ile Cooking 1
Type of Slow Cooker 2-3

II. CHICKEN

Chicken Tikka Masala 4
Moroccan Chicken 5
Lemon Garlic Chicken 6
Creamy Chicken and Mushroom Pasta 7
Chicken Cacciatore 8
White Chicken Chili 9
Chicken Paprikash 10
Creamy Tomato Basil Chicken 11
Honey Garlic Chicken 12
Mexican Chicken and Rice 13
Creamy Bacon Ranch Chicken 14
Thai Chicken Curry 15
Creamy Garlic Chicken and Potatoes 16
Chicken Tacos 17
Creamy Tomato Chicken 18
Chicken Enchiladas 19
BBQ Pulled Chicken 20
Chicken Alfredo 21
Chicken Fajitas 22
Chicken Noodle Soup 23
Chicken and Dumplings 24
Chicken Teriyaki 25

SLOW COOKER RECIPE BOOK

SLOW COOKER RECIPE BOOK
FOR 2 PEOPLES

TABLE OF CONTENTS

III. BEEF

Corned Beef and Cabbage	**26**
Beef and Vegetable Stew	**27**
Chili Beef	**28**
Meatballs	**29**
Beef Ragu	**30**
Beef Stew	**31**
Beef and Mushroom Stroganoff	**32**
Beef Bourguignon	**33**
Pot Roast	**34**
Spaghetti Bolognese	**35**
Slow Cooker Lasagna	**36**
Beef and Broccoli	**37**
Beef Stroganoff	**38**
Korean Beef Tacos	**39**
Beef and Guinness Stew	**40**
Beef Gyros	**41**

IV. SOUP

Spicy Chicken and Lentil Soup	**42**
Split Pea Soup	**43**
Italian Wedding Soup	**44**
Chicken and Wild Rice Soup	**45**
Ham and White Bean Soup	**46**
Beef and Barley Soup	**47**
Spicy Black Bean Soup	**48**
Lentil Soup	**49**

SLOW COOKER RECIPE BOOK

SLOW COOKER RECIPE BOOK
FOR 2 PEOPLES

TABLE OF CONTENTS

IV. SOUP

Tomato Basil Soup	**50**
Minestrone Soup	**51**

V. VEGETABLE

Vegetable Curry	**52**
Lentil and Vegetable Stew	**53**
Moroccan Vegetable Stew	**54**
Ratatouille	**55**
Sweet Potato and Black Bean Chili	**56**
Vegetarian Chili	**57**
Vegetarian Lasagna	**58**
Ratatouille with Chickpeas	**59**
Cheesy Broccoli and Rice Casserole	**60**

VI. PORK

Balsamic Pork Tenderloin	**61**
Sweet and Sour Pork	**62**
Pulled Pork	**63**
Pork Carnitas	**64**
Pork and Bean Chili	**65**
Cuban Mojo Pork	**66**
Pork Roast with Vegetables	**67**

VII. OTHER

Moroccan Lamb Stew	**68**
Sausage and Bean Casserole	**69**

SLOW COOKER RECIPE BOOK

INTRODUCTION

What is Slow Cooker

A slow cooker, commonly referred to as a crock-pot, is a type of electric kitchen device used to prepare food at a low temperature slowly. A ceramic or porcelain pot with an electric heating element surrounding it, as well as a lid, make up the slow cooker. To keep heat from escaping, the pot's cover is made to fit snugly. Meals that are tender and tasty are produced by the low and slow cooking technique, which allows the food to simmer gradually. Slow cookers are useful for hectic schedules since they enable hands-free cooking while you go about your day.

Soups, stews, roasts, casseroles, and other dishes that need to cook slowly are best prepared in slow cookers. They are also fantastic for families or busy people who want a hot, ready-to-eat meal at the end of the day without having to actively cook. Because they enable huge quantities of food to be cooked at once and then divided up for later consumption, slow cookers are especially excellent for batch cooking and meal preparation. Additionally, homemade broths and stocks can be created in slow cookers from scratch and then used in a variety of dishes.

Why Use a Slow Cooker while Cooking

Convenience
Using a slow cooker is quite easy. Once all the ingredients have been added, you may set the timer and let the food cook on its own. This frees you from having to worry about cooking as you go about your day. Meals made with slow cooking are rich and flavorful because the flavors of the components can melt together.

Meals that are healthier
Slow cooking allows you to use less oil and fat, it is a healthier method of cooking. The slow cooking method also aids in keeping the food's nutrients intact.

Cost-effective
Slow cookers are a good option for cooking because they consume less electricity than other cooking techniques. They use less electricity than an oven or stovetop, and the long cooking time allows the food to cook slowly and evenly without wasting energy. Plus, you can use cheaper cuts of meat in a slow cooker, which means you'll save money on your grocery bill.

Versatility
A range of foods, including stews, soups, casseroles, and even desserts, can be prepared in slow cookers. They work well for preparing tough meat slices that need a lot of time and slow cooking to become soft.

INTRODUCTION

Type of Slow Cooker

Basic Slow Cooker

- The most basic kind of slow cooker on the market is the manual model. The user must manually switch the heater on and off, and it normally has two heat levels, low and high. The food is cooked at a lower temperature for a longer time on the low setting, and at a higher temperature for a shorter time on the high setting. The cooking pot on manual slow cookers is often detachable and simple to clean. Additionally, they are typically more cheap than other slow cooker varieties. But because they lack any fancy features, they might not be up to more difficult cooking duties.

Programmable Slow Cooker

- With a slow cooker that can be programmed, you may set the temperature and cooking time for a predetermined amount of time. When that time is up, the slow cooker will automatically switch to the warm mode. For folks who are busy and want a ready-to-eat supper when they get home, this kind of slow cooker works nicely. Digital displays, numerous settings, including hot, low, and warm, as well as certain models' ability to sauté or sear are common characteristics of programmable slow cookers. With the help of the timer function, you can set the cooking timer for a specified amount of time. When that time is up, the slow cooker will automatically transition to the warm setting. This helps to avoid overcooking and maintain a safe temperature for the dish until it is time to serve.

Multi-Cooker

- A multi-cooker is a kitchen gadget that can handle multiple culinary tasks in one unit. It typically features a variety of cooking options, including steaming, sautéing, baking, pressure cooking, slow cooking, and more. A multi cooker's benefit is that it can replace multiple other kitchen equipment, saving you time and space. It can also be a terrific choice for individuals who wish to prepare a variety of foods without having to buy a number of different gadgets. Additionally, some models include extra features like delayed start and keep-warm capabilities that make planning and preparing meals easier.

Casserole Slow Cooker

- Casserole slow cookers are made for baking casseroles and other baked goods. For browning or sautéing ingredients before slow cooking, they typically contain a removable cooking pot that may be used in the oven or on the stovetop. Usually made of glass, the lid lets you look within without opening it and interfering with cooking. Slow cookers for casseroles frequently have bigger capacities than other slow cookers, making them perfect for meal preparation or feeding a large number of people. They are an adaptable addition to any kitchen because they can also be used to create bread or desserts.

INTRODUCTION

Travel Slow Cooker
- The typical slow cooker has been scaled down and made more portable as a "travel slow cooker." It normally weighs little and features handles and a lockable top for transport convenience. People who want to prepare meals at home and then bring them to work, potlucks, or other occasions should use this kind of slow cooker. In order to keep the food warm while being transported, some travel slow cookers even include insulated carrying cases.

Connectable Slow Cooker
- A slow cooker that can be connected to additional units to increase its cooking capacity is known as a connectable slow cooker. For those who might need to prepare large dinners for get-togethers with family and friends or other occasions, this is a practical solution. Connectable slow cookers can be connected into a single power outlet and often contain a locking mechanism that enables the units to securely link to one another. Some connectable slow cookers also include extra functions like temperature control and individual timer settings. This makes cooking more accurate and lowers the chance that the meal may be overcooked or undercooked.

Instant Pot
- An electric pressure cooker, slow cooker, rice cooker, steamer, yogurt maker, sauté/browning pan, and warming pot are all included in the Instant Pot multicooker. It swiftly and effectively cooks food while preserving its flavors and nutrients using pressured steam. The Instant Pot is a flexible kitchen device that can be used for a variety of dishes thanks to its many functions and cooking programs. It is a safe and practical alternative for cooking at home because it also contains safety features like a lid lock and overheat protection.

Slow Cooker Chicken Tikka Masala

CHICKEN

This classic Indian dish is perfect for a cozy night in. Serve with rice and naan bread.

Food Preparation: 20-30min | Cook Time: 4-6 hours | Yield: 2 servings

Ingredients:
- 2 chicken breasts, cut into bite-sized pieces
- 1 onion, diced
- 2 cloves garlic, minced
- 1 tbsp ginger, grated
- 1 tbsp garam masala
- 1 tsp paprika
- 1/2 tsp turmeric
- 1/2 tsp cumin
- 1/2 tsp coriander
- 1/4 tsp cayenne pepper (optional)
- 1 can (400g) diced tomatoes
- 1/2 cup plain yogurt
- Salt and pepper, to taste
- Fresh cilantro, chopped (optional)

Instructions:
1. In a large skillet, heat some oil over medium heat. Add the chicken and cook until browned on all sides.
2. Add the onion, garlic, and ginger and cook until the onion is softened, about 5 minutes.
3. Add the garam masala, paprika, turmeric, cumin, coriander, and cayenne pepper (if using) and stir to coat everything in the spices. Cook for an additional minute.
4. Transfer everything to the slow cooker.
5. Add the diced tomatoes, yogurt, and a pinch of salt and pepper. Stir everything together.
6. Cover the slow cooker and cook on low for 4-6 hours or high for 2-3 hours, until the chicken is cooked through and tender.
7. Serve the chicken tikka masala over rice, garnished with fresh cilantro (if desired).

CHICKEN

Moroccan Chicken

A flavorful dish with chicken, spices, apricots and almonds. Serve with couscous.

Food Preparation: 20-30min | Cook Time: 6-8 hours | Yield: 2 servings

Ingredients:
- 2 chicken breasts, boneless and skinless
- 1 onion, chopped
- 2 garlic cloves, minced
- 1 can (14 oz) diced tomatoes, undrained
- 1/2 cup chicken broth
- 1/2 cup pitted green olives
- 1/4 cup raisins
- 1 tbsp honey
- 1 tsp ground cumin
- 1 tsp ground coriander
- 1/2 tsp ground cinnamon
- Salt and pepper, to taste
- Chopped fresh parsley, for garnish

Instructions:
1. Heat a skillet over medium-high heat. Add the chicken breasts and cook until browned on both sides, about 3-4 minutes per side. Transfer the chicken to the slow cooker.
2. Add the onion and garlic to the same skillet. Cook until the vegetables are tender, stirring occasionally.
3. Add the cooked onion and garlic to the slow cooker.
4. Add the diced tomatoes (with their juice), chicken broth, green olives, raisins, honey, cumin, coriander, cinnamon, salt, and pepper to the slow cooker. Stir everything together.
5. Cover the slow cooker and cook on low for 6-8 hours or high for 3-4 hours, until the chicken is cooked through and tender.
6. Season the chicken and sauce with additional salt and pepper, to taste.
7. Serve the Moroccan Chicken hot, with couscous, rice, or quinoa, if desired. Garnish with chopped fresh parsley.

CHICKEN

Slow Cooker Lemon Garlic Chicken

Tender chicken breasts infused with lemon and garlic, served over rice or potatoes.

Food Preparation: 10-15min | Cook Time: 4-6 hours | Yield: 2 servings

Ingredients:
- 2 boneless, skinless chicken breasts
- 1/4 cup all-purpose flour
- Salt and pepper to taste
- 2 tablespoons olive oil
- 4 garlic cloves, minced
- 1/2 cup chicken broth
- 1/4 cup freshly squeezed lemon juice
- 2 tablespoons honey
- 1 teaspoon dried oregano
- 1 lemon, thinly sliced

Instructions:
1. Season the chicken breasts with salt and pepper, and coat them with flour.
2. In a large skillet over medium-high heat, heat the olive oil. Once hot, add the chicken and cook until browned on both sides, about 3-4 minutes per side.
3. Transfer the chicken to the slow cooker.
4. In the same skillet, add the minced garlic and cook for 1-2 minutes until fragrant.
5. Add the chicken broth, lemon juice, honey, and oregano, and stir until well combined.
6. Pour the mixture over the chicken in the slow cooker.
7. Top the chicken with the lemon slices.
8. Cover and cook on low for 4-5 hours or on high for 2-3 hours, until the chicken is cooked through and tender.
9. Serve the chicken with the sauce spooned over it, and enjoy!

Note: You can also add some vegetables, such as carrots or green beans, to the slow cooker if you like.

CHICKEN

Slow Cooker Creamy Chicken and Mushroom Pasta

A creamy and flavorful chicken and mushroom pasta dish made with white wine, garlic, and herbs.

Food Preparation: 10-15min | Cook Time: 3-6 hours | Yield: 2 servings

Ingredients:
- 2 boneless, skinless chicken breasts, cut into bite-sized pieces
- 1 cup sliced mushrooms
- 1/2 onion, diced
- 2 garlic cloves, minced
- 1/2 cup chicken broth
- 1/2 cup heavy cream
- 1/4 cup grated Parmesan cheese
- 1 tsp dried thyme
- Salt and pepper to taste
- 6 oz cooked pasta (such as linguine or fettuccine)
- Chopped parsley for garnish

Instructions:
1. In a slow cooker, add the chicken, mushrooms, onion, garlic, chicken broth, heavy cream, Parmesan cheese, thyme, salt, and pepper.
2. Stir until everything is well combined.
3. Cook on high for 2-3 hours or low for 4-6 hours.
4. When the chicken is fully cooked, stir in the cooked pasta and let it sit in the slow cooker for 5-10 minutes.
5. Serve hot, garnished with chopped parsley.

CHICKEN

Slow Cooker Chicken Cacciatore

Tender chicken cooked in a rich tomato-based sauce with mushrooms, onions, and peppers, served over pasta or rice.

Food Preparation: 15-20min | Cook Time: 4-8 hours | Yield: 2 servings

Ingredients:
- 2 boneless, skinless chicken breasts, cut into bite-sized pieces
- 1/2 onion, chopped
- 1/2 green bell pepper, chopped
- 2 cloves garlic, minced
- 1 can (14 oz) diced tomatoes, undrained
- 1/2 cup chicken broth
- 1/4 cup red wine
- 1 tsp dried basil
- 1/2 tsp dried oregano
- Salt and pepper, to taste
- 1/4 cup all-purpose flour
- 2 tbsp olive oil
- 1/4 cup pitted black olives
- 1/4 cup chopped fresh parsley

Instructions:
1. In a small bowl, mix together the flour, salt, and pepper. Dredge the chicken pieces in the flour mixture and shake off any excess.
2. Heat the olive oil in a skillet over medium-high heat. Add the chicken pieces and brown them on all sides, about 5-7 minutes.
3. Transfer the chicken to the slow cooker.
4. Add the onion, green bell pepper, garlic, diced tomatoes, chicken broth, red wine, basil, oregano, salt, and pepper to the slow cooker. Stir to combine.
5. Cover and cook on low for 6-8 hours or on high for 3-4 hours, or until the chicken is cooked through and tender.
6. Stir in the black olives and parsley.
7. Serve hot with pasta or crusty bread.

CHICKEN

Slow Cooker White Chicken Chili

A comforting and creamy chili made with chicken, white beans, and a blend of spices.

Food Preparation: 10-15min | Cook Time: 4-8 hours | Yield: 2 servings

Ingredients:
- 1 tablespoon olive oil
- 1 small onion, diced
- 2 cloves garlic, minced
- 1 small jalapeño pepper, seeded and minced
- 1/2 teaspoon ground cumin
- 1/2 teaspoon dried oregano
- 1/4 teaspoon ground coriander
- 1/4 teaspoon salt
- 1/8 teaspoon cayenne pepper
- 1 can (15 ounces) white beans, drained and rinsed
- 1 can (4 ounces) chopped green chilies
- 1 cup chicken broth
- 1/2 pound boneless, skinless chicken breasts
- 1/4 cup chopped fresh cilantro
- 1 tablespoon lime juice

Instructions:
1. Heat the olive oil in a skillet over medium heat. Add the onion and cook until softened, about 5 minutes. Add the garlic and jalapeño pepper and cook for 1 minute longer.
2. Add the cumin, oregano, coriander, salt, and cayenne pepper to the skillet and cook for 1 minute, stirring constantly.
3. Transfer the onion mixture to a 2-quart slow cooker. Add the white beans, green chilies, and chicken broth and stir to combine.
4. Place the chicken breasts on top of the bean mixture.
5. Cover the slow cooker and cook on low for 6-8 hours or on high for 3-4 hours, or until the chicken is cooked through.
6. Remove the chicken from the slow cooker and shred it using two forks. Return the shredded chicken to the slow cooker.
7. Stir in the cilantro and lime juice.
8. Serve hot with your desired toppings such as shredded cheese, sour cream, diced avocado, or tortilla chips.

CHICKEN

Slow Cooker Chicken Paprikash

Chicken thighs cooked in a paprika-infused tomato sauce with onions and peppers, served over rice or egg noodles.

Food Preparation: 15-20min | Cook Time: 3-6 hours | Yield: 2 servings

Ingredients:
- 2 chicken breasts, boneless and skinless
- 1 onion, diced
- 1 red bell pepper, diced
- 2 garlic cloves, minced
- 2 tbsp paprika
- 1 tsp salt
- 1/4 tsp black pepper
- 1/2 cup chicken broth
- 1/2 cup sour cream
- 2 tbsp cornstarch
- 2 tbsp water
- 2 cups cooked egg noodles, for serving
- Fresh parsley, chopped, for garnish

Instructions:
1. Place the chicken breasts in the bottom of a 2-quart slow cooker.
2. Add the diced onion, red bell pepper, minced garlic, paprika, salt, and black pepper on top of the chicken.
3. Pour chicken broth over everything.
4. Cover and cook on low for 6 hours or on high for 3 hours.
5. In a small bowl, whisk together the sour cream, cornstarch, and water until smooth.
6. Add the sour cream mixture to the slow cooker and stir gently.
7. Cover and cook on high for an additional 20-30 minutes, or until the sauce has thickened.
8. Serve over cooked egg noodles, garnished with fresh parsley.

CHICKEN

Slow Cooker Creamy Tomato Basil Chicken

Juicy chicken breasts cooked in a creamy tomato sauce with fresh basil, garlic, and Parmesan cheese, served over pasta or rice.

Food Preparation: 10-15min | Cook Time: 4-6 hours | Yield: 2 servings

Ingredients:
- 2 boneless, skinless chicken breasts
- 1 can diced tomatoes
- 1/2 cup chicken broth
- 1/4 cup heavy cream
- 1/4 cup chopped fresh basil
- 2 cloves garlic, minced
- Salt and pepper, to taste

Instructions:
1. Place the chicken breasts in the slow cooker.
2. In a small bowl, mix together the diced tomatoes, chicken broth, heavy cream, basil, garlic, salt, and pepper.
3. Pour the tomato mixture over the chicken in the slow cooker.
4. Cover and cook on low for 4-6 hours, or until the chicken is cooked through and tender.
5. Shred the chicken with two forks, and stir it back into the sauce.
6. Serve hot over rice, pasta, or your favorite grain.

Slow Cooker Honey Garlic Chicken

CHICKEN

Juicy and tender chicken thighs in a sweet and garlicky sauce, served over rice or noodles.

Food Preparation: 10-15min | Cook Time: 4-6 hours | Yield: 2 servings

Ingredients:
- 2 boneless, skinless chicken breasts
- 1/4 cup honey
- 1/4 cup soy sauce
- 2 tablespoons ketchup
- 2 cloves garlic, minced
- 1/4 teaspoon dried oregano
- 1/4 teaspoon dried basil
- 1/4 teaspoon black pepper
- 1 tablespoon cornstarch
- 1 tablespoon cold water
- Sesame seeds and sliced green onions, for garnish (optional)

Instructions:
1. In a small bowl, whisk together the honey, soy sauce, ketchup, garlic, oregano, basil, and black pepper.
2. Place the chicken breasts in the slow cooker and pour the honey garlic mixture over them, making sure the chicken is coated evenly.
3. Cook on low for 4-6 hours, or until the chicken is cooked through and tender.
4. In a small bowl, whisk together the cornstarch and cold water until smooth. Stir the cornstarch mixture into the sauce in the slow cooker and cook on high for an additional 15-30 minutes, or until the sauce has thickened.
5. Serve the chicken with the sauce spooned over it, garnished with sesame seeds and sliced green onions if desired. Enjoy!

CHICKEN

Slow Cooker Mexican Chicken and Rice

Juicy chicken cooked with Mexican spices, rice, beans, and corn, perfect for a filling and flavorful meal.

Food Preparation: 10-15min | Cook Time: 4-7 hours | Yield: 2 servings

Ingredients:
- 2 boneless, skinless chicken breasts
- 1 cup uncooked white rice
- 1 cup canned black beans, drained and rinsed
- 1 cup frozen corn
- 1 cup salsa
- 1 cup chicken broth
- 1 tsp chili powder
- 1/2 tsp cumin
- 1/4 tsp garlic powder
- Salt and pepper to taste
- Chopped fresh cilantro for garnish (optional)

Instructions:
1. Place the chicken breasts in the bottom of the slow cooker.
2. Add the uncooked rice, black beans, corn, salsa, chicken broth, chili powder, cumin, garlic powder, salt, and pepper to the slow cooker.
3. Stir everything together until well combined.
4. Cook on low for 6-7 hours or on high for 3-4 hours, or until the chicken is cooked through and the rice is tender.
5. Remove the chicken from the slow cooker and shred it with a fork.
6. Return the shredded chicken to the slow cooker and stir everything together.
7. Serve hot, garnished with fresh cilantro if desired.

CHICKEN

Slow Cooker Creamy Bacon Ranch Chicken

Juicy chicken breasts cooked in a creamy and savory bacon ranch sauce, perfect for a satisfying and easy dinner.

Food Preparation: 10-15min | Cook Time: 4-7 hours | Yield: 2 servings

Ingredients:
- 2 boneless, skinless chicken breasts
- 4 slices of bacon, cooked and crumbled
- 1 packet ranch seasoning mix
- 1/2 cup chicken broth
- 1/2 cup heavy cream
- 1/2 cup shredded cheddar cheese
- 1/4 cup chopped fresh parsley

Instructions:
1. Place the chicken breasts in the bottom of a slow cooker.
2. Sprinkle the ranch seasoning mix evenly over the chicken.
3. Pour the chicken broth into the slow cooker.
4. Cover and cook on low for 6-7 hours or on high for 3-4 hours, or until the chicken is tender and fully cooked.
5. Remove the chicken from the slow cooker and shred it with two forks.
6. In a small saucepan, heat the heavy cream over medium heat until it comes to a simmer.
7. Stir in the shredded cheddar cheese until it is fully melted and the sauce is smooth.
8. Pour the cheese sauce over the shredded chicken and stir to combine.
9. Top the chicken with the crumbled bacon and chopped parsley.
10. Serve hot and enjoy!

Note: You can also add cooked pasta or rice to the slow cooker during the last 30 minutes of cooking to make this a complete meal.

CHICKEN

Slow Cooker Thai Chicken Curry

A flavorful and spicy Thai-inspired chicken curry with vegetables, coconut milk, and curry paste, served over rice or noodles.

Food Preparation: 15-20min | Cook Time: 3-6 hours | Yield: 2 servings

Ingredients:
- 2 boneless, skinless chicken breasts, cut into bite-sized pieces
- 1 red bell pepper, sliced
- 1 onion, chopped
- 2 garlic cloves, minced
- 1 tablespoon grated fresh ginger
- 1 tablespoon red curry paste
- 1 tablespoon brown sugar
- 1 tablespoon fish sauce
- 1 can (14 oz) coconut milk
- Salt and pepper, to taste
- Juice of 1 lime
- Fresh cilantro, chopped, for garnish
- Cooked rice or noodles, for serving

Instructions:
1. In a slow cooker, combine the chicken, red bell pepper, onion, garlic, ginger, red curry paste, brown sugar, fish sauce, and coconut milk. Season with salt and pepper, to taste.
2. Stir well to combine all ingredients.
3. Cover and cook on LOW for 4-6 hours or HIGH for 2-3 hours, or until the chicken is cooked through and tender.
4. Stir in lime juice.
5. Serve the curry hot, over cooked rice or noodles, and garnished with fresh cilantro.

CHICKEN

Slow Cooker Creamy Garlic Chicken and Potatoes

Tender chicken and potatoes in a creamy and garlicky sauce.

Food Preparation: 10-15min | Cook Time: 4-8 hours | Yield: 2 servings

Ingredients:
- 2 boneless, skinless chicken breasts
- 2 cups baby potatoes, quartered
- 1 cup chicken broth
- 1/2 cup heavy cream
- 3 cloves garlic, minced
- 1 tsp dried thyme
- 1/2 tsp salt
- 1/4 tsp black pepper
- 1 tbsp cornstarch
- 1 tbsp water
- Fresh parsley for garnish

Instructions:
1. In a slow cooker, combine chicken, potatoes, chicken broth, heavy cream, garlic, thyme, salt, and pepper.
2. Cover and cook on low for 6-8 hours or on high for 3-4 hours, or until chicken is cooked through and potatoes are tender.
3. In a small bowl, whisk together cornstarch and water until smooth. Add to the slow cooker and stir until the sauce thickens.
4. Serve hot, garnished with fresh parsley.

Note: You can add other vegetables such as carrots, green beans or mushrooms to the stew if desired.

CHICKEN

Slow Cooker Chicken Tacos

Tender and juicy chicken tacos made in the slow cooker with your favorite taco toppings.

Food Preparation: 10-15min | Cook Time: 4-8 hours | Yield: 2 servings

Ingredients:
- 2 boneless, skinless chicken breasts
- 1/2 cup salsa
- 1 tbsp taco seasoning
- Salt and pepper, to taste
- 4-6 small corn tortillas
- Optional toppings: diced tomato, diced onion, shredded lettuce, shredded cheese, sour cream

Instructions:
1. Place the chicken breasts in a small slow cooker and season with salt and pepper.
2. Pour the salsa over the chicken and sprinkle with taco seasoning.
3. Cover and cook on low for 6-8 hours or on high for 3-4 hours, until the chicken is cooked through and tender.
4. Use two forks to shred the chicken and mix it with the salsa and taco seasoning in the slow cooker.
5. Warm the tortillas according to package instructions and spoon the chicken mixture onto each tortilla.
6. Top with desired toppings, such as diced tomato, diced onion, shredded lettuce, shredded cheese, and sour cream.

CHICKEN

Slow Cooker Creamy Tomato Chicken

A comforting and creamy chicken dish made with canned tomatoes, cream cheese, and Italian seasoning.

Food Preparation: 10-15min | Cook Time: 3-6 hours | Yield: 2 servings

Ingredients:
- 2 boneless, skinless chicken breasts
- 1 can (14.5 oz) diced tomatoes, undrained
- 1/2 cup heavy cream
- 1/2 cup chicken broth
- 1 tsp dried basil
- 1 tsp dried oregano
- 1 tsp garlic powder
- 1/2 tsp salt
- 1/4 tsp black pepper
- 2 tbsp cornstarch
- 2 tbsp water
- Fresh parsley, chopped (optional)

Instructions:
1. Add the chicken breasts to a small slow cooker.
2. In a separate bowl, whisk together the diced tomatoes (undrained), heavy cream, chicken broth, dried basil, dried oregano, garlic powder, salt, and pepper.
3. Pour the tomato mixture over the chicken in the slow cooker.
4. Cover and cook on low for 4-6 hours or on high for 2-3 hours, until the chicken is cooked through and tender.
5. In a small bowl, whisk together the cornstarch and water until smooth.
6. Remove the chicken from the slow cooker and set aside.
7. Whisk the cornstarch mixture into the tomato sauce in the slow cooker.
8. Cover and cook on high for an additional 15-20 minutes, until the sauce has thickened.
9. Shred the chicken with a fork and return it to the slow cooker.
10. Stir to combine the chicken with the creamy tomato sauce.
11. Serve hot and garnish with chopped fresh parsley (optional).

Note: This Slow Cooker Creamy Tomato Chicken goes well with rice, pasta, or crusty bread. You can also add some vegetables, such as chopped bell peppers, mushrooms, or spinach, to the tomato sauce for extra flavor and nutrition.

CHICKEN

Chicken Enchiladas

Delicious and cheesy with chicken, tortillas and sauce. Serve with rice and beans.

Food Preparation: 20-25min | Cook Time: 4-8 hours | Yield: 2 servings

Ingredients:
- 2 boneless, skinless chicken breasts
- 1 can of enchilada sauce
- 1/2 onion, chopped
- 1 garlic clove, minced
- 1 tsp chili powder
- 1/2 tsp ground cumin
- Salt and pepper, to taste
- 4-6 small flour tortillas
- 1/2 cup shredded cheddar cheese
- Fresh cilantro, chopped, for serving (optional)

Instructions:
1. Place the chicken breasts in the slow cooker. Pour the enchilada sauce over the chicken.
2. Add the chopped onion, minced garlic, chili powder, ground cumin, salt, and pepper to the slow cooker. Stir everything together.
3. Cover the slow cooker and cook on low for 6-8 hours or on high for 3-4 hours, until the chicken is cooked through and tender.
4. Remove the chicken from the slow cooker and shred it with two forks.
5. Preheat the oven to 375°F.
6. In a baking dish, spread a thin layer of enchilada sauce on the bottom.
7. Place a tortilla on a flat surface and spoon some shredded chicken and a little bit of enchilada sauce onto the center of the tortilla. Roll up the tortilla and place it seam-side down in the baking dish. Repeat with the remaining tortillas and chicken.
8. Pour the remaining enchilada sauce over the tortillas in the baking dish. Sprinkle the shredded cheddar cheese over the top.
9. Cover the baking dish with foil and bake in the preheated oven for 20-25 minutes, until the cheese is melted and bubbly.
10. Serve the chicken enchiladas with chopped fresh cilantro, if desired.

Slow Cooker BBQ Pulled Chicken

CHICKEN

Juicy and flavorful shredded chicken in a smoky BBQ sauce, perfect for sandwiches or served over rice.

Food Preparation: 10-15min | Cook Time: 4-8 hours | Yield: 2 servings

Ingredients:
- 2 boneless, skinless chicken breasts
- 1/2 cup BBQ sauce
- 1/4 cup chicken broth
- 1 tbsp Worcestershire sauce
- 1 tbsp brown sugar
- 1 tsp smoked paprika
- 1/2 tsp garlic powder
- Salt and pepper, to taste
- Sandwich rolls, for serving

Instructions:
1. In a small bowl, whisk together the BBQ sauce, chicken broth, Worcestershire sauce, brown sugar, smoked paprika, garlic powder, salt, and pepper.
2. Place the chicken breasts in the slow cooker and pour the BBQ sauce mixture over the top, making sure the chicken is coated.
3. Cover and cook on low for 6-8 hours or on high for 3-4 hours, until the chicken is tender and easily shreds.
4. Shred the chicken with two forks and stir it into the sauce in the slow cooker.
5. Serve the pulled chicken on sandwich rolls, topped with extra BBQ sauce if desired.

CHICKEN

Slow Cooker Chicken Alfredo

Creamy and delicious with chicken and pasta. Serve with garlic bread.

Food Preparation: 10-15min | Cook Time: 4-8 hours | Yield: 2 servings

Ingredients:
- 2 boneless, skinless chicken breasts
- 1/2 pound fettuccine pasta
- 2 cups chicken broth
- 1 cup heavy cream
- 1/2 cup grated Parmesan cheese
- 2 garlic cloves, minced
- 2 tbsp butter
- 1 tbsp all-purpose flour
- 1/2 tsp dried parsley
- Salt and pepper, to taste

Instructions:
1. Add the chicken breasts to the slow cooker. Pour the chicken broth over the chicken. Cover the slow cooker and cook on high for 3-4 hours or on low for 6-8 hours, until the chicken is tender and cooked through.
2. Remove the cooked chicken from the slow cooker and shred it with two forks. Discard any excess liquid from the slow cooker.
3. Cook the fettuccine pasta according to the package directions until al dente. Drain the pasta and set aside.
4. In a small saucepan, melt the butter over medium heat. Whisk in the flour and minced garlic, and cook for 1-2 minutes until the mixture turns golden brown.
5. Pour the butter and flour mixture into the slow cooker with the cooked chicken. Add the heavy cream, grated Parmesan cheese, dried parsley, salt, and pepper to the slow cooker. Stir everything together.
6. Cover the slow cooker and cook on high for 30-45 minutes, until the sauce has thickened.
7. Serve the Slow Cooker Chicken Alfredo hot, over cooked fettuccine pasta.

Chicken Fajitas

CHICKEN

Tender chicken, peppers and onions cooked in a flavorful sauce. Serve with tortillas.

Food Preparation: 15-20min | Cook Time: 2-4 hours | Yield: 2 servings

Ingredients:
- 1 lb boneless, skinless chicken breasts, sliced into strips
- 1/2 onion, sliced
- 1 red bell pepper, sliced
- 1 green bell pepper, sliced
- 2 cloves garlic, minced
- 2 tsp chili powder
- 1 tsp ground cumin
- 1/2 tsp smoked paprika
- 1/2 tsp salt
- 1/4 tsp black pepper
- 1 tbsp olive oil
- Flour tortillas, for serving
- Salsa, sour cream, guacamole, shredded cheese, and chopped cilantro, for serving (optional)

Instructions:
1. In a small bowl, mix together the chili powder, cumin, smoked paprika, salt, and black pepper. Set aside.
2. Heat the olive oil in a large skillet over medium-high heat. Add the chicken strips and cook until browned on all sides, about 5-7 minutes.
3. Add the sliced onion, red bell pepper, green bell pepper, and minced garlic to the skillet with the chicken. Sprinkle the spice mixture over the vegetables and chicken, and toss everything together.
4. Transfer the chicken and vegetable mixture to the slow cooker. Cover the slow cooker and cook on low for 3-4 hours or on high for 1-2 hours, until the chicken is cooked through and the vegetables are tender.
5. Warm the flour tortillas according to the package directions. Serve the chicken fajitas with the warm tortillas, and toppings like salsa, sour cream, guacamole, shredded cheese, and chopped cilantro, if desired.

CHICKEN

Chicken Noodle Soup

A classic comfort food made with chicken, noodles and vegetables. Serve with crackers.

Food Preparation: 10-15min | Cook Time: 4-8 hours | Yield: 2 servings

Ingredients:
- 2 boneless, skinless chicken breasts
- 1/2 onion, chopped
- 2 garlic cloves, minced
- 2 carrots, peeled and sliced
- 2 celery stalks, sliced
- 4 cups chicken broth
- 1 tsp dried thyme
- 1 tsp dried parsley
- Salt and pepper, to taste
- 1 cup egg noodles
- Fresh parsley, chopped, for serving (optional)

Instructions:
1. Add the chicken breasts, chopped onion, minced garlic, sliced carrots, sliced celery, chicken broth, dried thyme, dried parsley, salt, and pepper to the slow cooker.
2. Stir everything together, cover the slow cooker, and cook on low for 6-8 hours or on high for 3-4 hours.
3. In the last 30 minutes of cooking, add the egg noodles to the slow cooker. Stir everything together and continue cooking until the noodles are tender.
4. Remove the chicken breasts from the slow cooker and shred the meat using two forks.
5. Return the shredded chicken to the slow cooker and stir everything together.
6. Serve the chicken noodle soup with chopped fresh parsley, if desired.

CHICKEN

Chicken and Dumplings

Comfort food at its best! Slow-cooked chicken with fluffy dumplings and vegetables.

Food Preparation: 10-15min | Cook Time: 4-8 hours | Yield: 2 servings

Ingredients:
- 1 boneless, skinless chicken breast, cut into bite-sized pieces
- 1/2 onion, diced
- 2 carrots, peeled and sliced
- 2 celery stalks, sliced
- 2 garlic cloves, minced
- 1/2 tsp dried thyme
- 1 bay leaf
- 2 cups chicken broth
- 1/2 cup milk
- 1 tbsp cornstarch
- Salt and pepper, to taste
- 1 cup flour
- 1 tsp baking powder
- 1/4 tsp salt
- 1/4 cup milk
- 2 tbsp butter, melted

Instructions:
1. Place the chicken, onion, carrots, celery, garlic, thyme, bay leaf, and chicken broth in the slow cooker.
2. Cover the slow cooker and cook on low for 6-8 hours or high for 3-4 hours, until the chicken is cooked through and the vegetables are tender.
3. Remove the bay leaf from the slow cooker.
4. In a separate bowl, whisk together the milk and cornstarch. Stir the mixture into the slow cooker and cook on high for an additional 15-20 minutes, until the broth has thickened.
5. In a separate bowl, whisk together the flour, baking powder, and salt. Stir in the milk and melted butter until a sticky dough forms.
6. Drop spoonfuls of the dough onto the surface of the hot chicken mixture in the slow cooker. Cover the slow cooker and cook on high for an additional 30 minutes, until the dumplings are cooked through.
7. Season the chicken and dumplings with salt and pepper, to taste.
8. Serve the chicken and dumplings hot, garnished with fresh parsley, if desired.

CHICKEN

Slow Cooker Chicken Teriyaki

Tender and flavorful chicken thighs in a sweet and savory teriyaki sauce, served over rice.

Food Preparation: 10-15min | Cook Time: 3-5 hours | Yield: 2 servings

Ingredients:
- 2 boneless, skinless chicken breasts
- 1/4 cup soy sauce
- 1/4 cup honey
- 2 tablespoons rice vinegar
- 1/4 teaspoon ground ginger
- 1/4 teaspoon garlic powder
- 1/4 cup cold water
- 2 tablespoons cornstarch
- Green onions, chopped, for garnish
- Sesame seeds, for garnish
- Cooked rice, for serving

Instructions:
1. In a small bowl, whisk together soy sauce, honey, rice vinegar, ginger, and garlic powder.
2. Place chicken breasts in the slow cooker and pour the sauce over the chicken.
3. Cover and cook on low for 4-5 hours or high for 2-3 hours, or until the chicken is cooked through and tender.
4. In a small bowl, whisk together cold water and cornstarch until smooth. Add to the slow cooker and stir well to combine.
5. Cook on high for an additional 30 minutes, or until the sauce has thickened.
6. Serve chicken over cooked rice and garnish with green onions and sesame seeds. Enjoy!

Corned Beef and Cabbage

A traditional Irish dish that's perfect for St. Patrick's Day or any time of year.

Food Preparation: 15-20min | Cook Time: 6-10 hours | Yield: 2 servings

Ingredients:
- 1 lb corned beef brisket
- 2 cups water
- 2 garlic cloves, minced
- 1 onion, peeled and chopped
- 1 bay leaf
- 1/2 head of cabbage, chopped into chunks
- 3 carrots, peeled and sliced
- 3 potatoes, peeled and chopped
- Salt and pepper, to taste

Instructions:
1. Rinse the corned beef brisket under cold water and pat it dry with paper towels.
2. Place the corned beef brisket in the slow cooker.
3. Add the water, garlic, onion, and bay leaf to the slow cooker.
4. Cover the slow cooker and cook on low for 8-10 hours or high for 4-6 hours, until the corned beef is tender.
5. Remove the corned beef from the slow cooker and place it on a cutting board. Cover the corned beef with foil to keep it warm.
6. Add the cabbage, carrots, and potatoes to the slow cooker. Stir everything together.
7. Cover the slow cooker and cook on high for an additional 1-2 hours, until the vegetables are tender.
8. Slice the corned beef against the grain into thin slices.
9. Season the vegetables with salt and pepper, to taste.
10. Serve the corned beef and vegetables hot, with mustard or horseradish sauce on the side.

BEEF

Slow Cooker Beef and Vegetable Stew

A comforting and flavorful stew made with beef, veggies, and a blend of spices.

Food Preparation: 15-20min | Cook Time: 4-8 hours | Yield: 2 servings

Ingredients:
- 1/2 pound beef chuck roast, cut into cubes
- 1 tablespoon olive oil
- 1 small onion, diced
- 2 garlic cloves, minced
- 2 cups beef broth
- 1 tablespoon tomato paste
- 1/2 teaspoon dried thyme
- 1/2 teaspoon dried rosemary
- 1/2 teaspoon salt
- 1/4 teaspoon black pepper
- 2 small potatoes, peeled and diced
- 1 cup chopped carrots
- 1 cup chopped celery
- 1 cup frozen peas
- 1 tablespoon cornstarch
- 1 tablespoon cold water

Instructions:
1. Heat the olive oil in a large skillet over medium-high heat. Add the beef cubes and cook until browned on all sides, about 5 minutes.
2. Transfer the beef to the slow cooker. Add the onion and garlic to the skillet and cook until softened, about 3 minutes. Transfer the onion and garlic to the slow cooker.
3. Add the beef broth, tomato paste, thyme, rosemary, salt, and black pepper to the slow cooker and stir to combine.
4. Add the diced potatoes, carrots, and celery to the slow cooker and stir to combine.
5. Cover and cook on low for 6-8 hours or high for 3-4 hours.
6. In a small bowl, whisk together the cornstarch and cold water until smooth. Stir the cornstarch mixture and the frozen peas into the stew. Cover and cook on high for an additional 15-20 minutes, or until the stew has thickened and the peas are heated through.
7. Serve hot and enjoy your Slow Cooker Beef and Vegetable Stew!

Slow Cooker Chili Beef

A classic recipe with ground beef, beans and chili powder. Serve with sour cream, cheese and tortilla chips.

Food Preparation: 15-20min | Cook Time: 4-8 hours | Yield: 2 servings

Ingredients:
- 1/2 lb ground beef
- 1/2 onion, diced
- 1 red bell pepper, diced
- 1 jalapeño pepper, seeded and diced
- 2 garlic cloves, minced
- 1 can (14 oz) diced tomatoes, undrained
- 1 can (8 oz) tomato sauce
- 1 can (15 oz) kidney beans, drained and rinsed
- 1 tbsp chili powder
- 1 tsp cumin
- 1/2 tsp smoked paprika
- 1/2 tsp dried oregano
- Salt and pepper, to taste

Instructions:
1. Heat a skillet over medium heat. Add the ground beef and cook until browned, breaking it up into small pieces with a wooden spoon.
2. Add the onion, red bell pepper, jalapeño pepper, and garlic to the skillet. Cook until the vegetables are tender, stirring occasionally.
3. Transfer the cooked beef and vegetables to the slow cooker.
4. Add the diced tomatoes, tomato sauce, kidney beans, chili powder, cumin, smoked paprika, oregano, salt, and pepper to the slow cooker. Stir everything together.
5. Cover the slow cooker and cook on low for 6-8 hours or high for 3-4 hours, until the chili is hot and the flavors have melded together.
6. Season the chili with additional salt and pepper, to taste.
7. Serve the chili hot, topped with shredded cheddar cheese, chopped green onions, and/or sour cream, if desired.

BEEF

Slow Cooker Meatballs

Juicy meatballs in a tomato sauce. Serve with spaghetti.

Food Preparation: 10-15min | Cook Time: 4-8 hours | Yield: 2 servings

Ingredients:
- 1 pound ground beef
- 1/2 onion, chopped
- 2 garlic cloves, minced
- 1/2 cup breadcrumbs
- 1/4 cup milk
- 1 egg, beaten
- 1 tsp dried oregano
- Salt and pepper, to taste
- 1 can of crushed tomatoes
- 1 tbsp tomato paste
- 1 tsp dried basil
- Fresh parsley, chopped, for serving (optional)

Instructions:
1. In a large bowl, mix together the ground beef, chopped onion, minced garlic, breadcrumbs, milk, beaten egg, dried oregano, salt, and pepper. Mix everything together until well combined.
2. Shape the meat mixture into small meatballs, about 1-2 inches in diameter.
3. Add the meatballs to the slow cooker.
4. In a small bowl, whisk together the crushed tomatoes, tomato paste, dried basil, salt, and pepper. Pour the mixture over the meatballs in the slow cooker.
5. Cover the slow cooker and cook on low for 6-8 hours or on high for 3-4 hours, until the meatballs are cooked through.
6. Serve the meatballs with the tomato sauce and chopped fresh parsley, if desired.

Slow Cooker Beef Ragu

Slow-cooked beef in a rich tomato-based sauce served over pasta, polenta, or mashed potatoes.

Food Preparation: 10-15min | Cook Time: 6-8 hours | Yield: 2 servings

BEEF

Ingredients:
- 1 pound beef chuck roast, trimmed and cut into 1-inch cubes
- 1 tablespoon olive oil
- 1/2 onion, diced
- 2 garlic cloves, minced
- 1/2 cup beef broth
- 1/2 cup red wine
- 1 can (14.5 ounces) crushed tomatoes
- 2 tablespoons tomato paste
- 1 teaspoon dried basil
- 1 teaspoon dried oregano
- Salt and pepper, to taste
- 4 ounces spaghetti or your preferred pasta, cooked according to package instructions
- Freshly grated Parmesan cheese, for serving
- Chopped fresh parsley, for garnish

Instructions:
1. Heat olive oil in a large skillet over medium-high heat. Add beef and brown on all sides, about 6-8 minutes. Transfer to a slow cooker.
2. In the same skillet, add onion and garlic and cook until softened, about 3-5 minutes. Add beef broth, red wine, crushed tomatoes, tomato paste, basil, and oregano. Stir to combine.
3. Pour mixture over beef in the slow cooker. Season with salt and pepper to taste.
4. Cover and cook on low for 6-8 hours, or until beef is tender and sauce is thickened.
5. Serve over cooked spaghetti or your preferred pasta. Sprinkle with freshly grated Parmesan cheese and chopped parsley.

BEEF

Beef Stew

A hearty and comforting stew with tender beef, vegetables and potatoes. Serve with crusty bread.

Food Preparation: 20-30min | Cook Time: 4-8 hours | Yield: 2 servings

Ingredients:

- 1/2 pound stew beef, cut into bite-sized pieces
- 1 onion, diced
- 2 garlic cloves, minced
- 2 medium carrots, peeled and sliced
- 2 medium potatoes, peeled and chopped
- 1/2 cup beef broth
- 1/2 cup red wine
- 1 tbsp tomato paste
- 1 tbsp Worcestershire sauce
- 1 tsp dried thyme
- Salt and pepper, to taste
- 1 tbsp cornstarch (optional)
- 1 tbsp water (optional)

Instructions:

1. Place the beef, onion, garlic, carrots, and potatoes into the slow cooker.
2. In a separate bowl, whisk together the beef broth, red wine, tomato paste, Worcestershire sauce, thyme, salt, and pepper. Pour the mixture over the beef and vegetables in the slow cooker.
3. Cover the slow cooker and cook on low for 6-8 hours or high for 3-4 hours, until the beef is tender and the vegetables are cooked through.
4. If you'd like a thicker stew, whisk together the cornstarch and water in a small bowl. Stir the mixture into the slow cooker and cook on high for an additional 30 minutes, until the stew has thickened.
5. Serve the beef stew hot with crusty bread or rolls, if desired.

Slow Cooker Beef and Mushroom Stroganoff

BEEF

Tender beef and earthy mushrooms in a rich and creamy sauce served over egg noodles.

Food Preparation: 15-20min | Cook Time: 4-8 hours | Yield: 2 servings

Ingredients:
- 1/2 pound beef stew meat
- 1/2 onion, diced
- 1 garlic clove, minced
- 1 cup sliced mushrooms
- 1/2 cup beef broth
- 1 tablespoon Worcestershire sauce
- 1/2 teaspoon dried thyme
- 1/2 teaspoon salt
- 1/4 teaspoon black pepper
- 1/4 cup sour cream
- 1 tablespoon cornstarch
- 1 tablespoon water
- Cooked egg noodles, for serving

Instructions:
1. In a 2-quart slow cooker, combine the beef stew meat, onion, garlic, mushrooms, beef broth, Worcestershire sauce, thyme, salt, and pepper. Stir to combine.
2. Cover and cook on low for 6-8 hours or until the beef is tender.
3. In a small bowl, whisk together the sour cream, cornstarch, and water until smooth. Stir the mixture into the slow cooker.
4. Cover and cook on high for an additional 15-20 minutes, or until the sauce has thickened.
5. Serve the beef stroganoff over cooked egg noodles.

BEEF

Beef Bourguignon

A French classic made with beef, vegetables and red wine. Serve with crusty bread.

Food Preparation: 25-30min | Cook Time: 4-8 hours | Yield: 2 servings

Ingredients:
- 1 lb beef chuck, cut into 1-inch cubes
- 1/2 onion, chopped
- 2 garlic cloves, minced
- 1 carrot, peeled and chopped
- 1/2 cup red wine
- 1 cup beef broth
- 1 tbsp tomato paste
- 1 tsp dried thyme
- 2 bay leaves
- Salt and pepper, to taste
- 8 oz button mushrooms, quartered
- 2 tbsp butter
- 2 tbsp all-purpose flour
- Fresh parsley, chopped, for serving (optional)

Instructions:
1. Heat a large skillet over medium-high heat. Add the beef cubes and brown on all sides, about 5-7 minutes. Transfer the beef to the slow cooker.
2. Add the chopped onion, minced garlic, and chopped carrot to the skillet. Cook, stirring occasionally, until the vegetables are softened, about 5 minutes.
3. Pour the red wine into the skillet with the vegetables and scrape up any browned bits from the bottom of the pan. Add the beef broth, tomato paste, dried thyme, bay leaves, salt, and pepper to the skillet. Bring the mixture to a simmer.
4. Pour the vegetable and wine mixture over the beef in the slow cooker. Stir everything together, cover the slow cooker, and cook on low for 6-8 hours or on high for 3-4 hours.
5. In the last 30 minutes of cooking, melt the butter in a small saucepan over medium heat. Whisk in the flour to create a roux. Cook, whisking constantly, for 2-3 minutes, until the roux is lightly browned.
6. Add the quartered mushrooms to the slow cooker and stir to combine. Slowly pour the roux into the slow cooker, stirring constantly. Cook for an additional 30 minutes, until the sauce has thickened.
7. Discard the bay leaves and serve the beef bourguignon over egg noodles, mashed potatoes, or crusty bread. Garnish with chopped fresh parsley, if desired.

BEEF

Slow Cooker Pot Roast

Tender beef slow-cooked with vegetables and potatoes. Serve with gravy.

Food Preparation: 15-20min | Cook Time: 4-8 hours | Yield: 2 servings

Ingredients:
- 1 lb beef chuck roast
- 1/2 onion, chopped
- 2 garlic cloves, minced
- 2 carrots, peeled and chopped
- 2 celery stalks, chopped
- 1 cup beef broth
- 1 tbsp tomato paste
- 1 tsp dried thyme
- 2 bay leaves
- Salt and pepper, to taste
- 2 tbsp all-purpose flour
- 2 tbsp butter
- Fresh parsley, chopped, for serving (optional)

Instructions:
1. Season the beef chuck roast generously with salt and pepper.
2. Heat a large skillet over medium-high heat. Add a little oil and brown the beef on all sides, about 5-7 minutes. Transfer the beef to the slow cooker.
3. Add the chopped onion, minced garlic, chopped carrots, and chopped celery to the skillet. Cook, stirring occasionally, until the vegetables are softened, about 5 minutes.
4. Pour the beef broth into the skillet with the vegetables and scrape up any browned bits from the bottom of the pan. Add the tomato paste, dried thyme, bay leaves, salt, and pepper to the skillet. Bring the mixture to a simmer.
5. Pour the vegetable and broth mixture over the beef in the slow cooker. Stir everything together, cover the slow cooker, and cook on low for 6-8 hours or on high for 3-4 hours.
6. In the last 30 minutes of cooking, melt the butter in a small saucepan over medium heat. Whisk in the flour to create a roux. Cook, whisking constantly, for 2-3 minutes, until the roux is lightly browned.
7. Slowly pour the roux into the slow cooker, stirring constantly. Cook for an additional 30 minutes, until the sauce has thickened.
8. Discard the bay leaves and serve the pot roast with the vegetables and sauce. Garnish with chopped fresh parsley, if desired.

BEEF

Spaghetti Bolognese

A classic Italian dish made with ground beef, tomatoes and pasta. Serve with garlic bread.

Food Preparation: 20-30min | Cook Time: 4-8 hours | Yield: 2 servings

Ingredients:
- 1/2 lb ground beef
- 1/2 onion, chopped
- 2 garlic cloves, minced
- 1 can (14 oz) diced tomatoes
- 1/2 cup tomato sauce
- 1 tsp dried oregano
- 1/2 tsp dried basil
- Salt and pepper, to taste
- 4 oz spaghetti
- Parmesan cheese, grated, for serving

Instructions:
1. Heat a large skillet over medium-high heat. Add the ground beef, chopped onion, and minced garlic. Cook, stirring occasionally, until the beef is browned and the onion is softened, about 5-7 minutes.
2. Add the diced tomatoes, tomato sauce, dried oregano, dried basil, salt, and pepper to the skillet with the beef mixture. Stir everything together and bring the sauce to a simmer.
3. Transfer the sauce to the slow cooker. Cover the slow cooker and cook on low for 6-8 hours or on high for 3-4 hours, until the sauce is thick and flavorful.
4. About 15 minutes before serving, cook the spaghetti according to the package directions until al dente. Drain the spaghetti and serve it with the Bolognese sauce.
5. Sprinkle grated Parmesan cheese on top of the Spaghetti Bolognese, if desired.

Slow Cooker Lasagna

Layered with pasta, meat sauce and cheese. A delicious and easy recipe.

Food Preparation: 30-40min | Cook Time: 3-6 hours | Yield: 2 servings

BEEF

Ingredients:
- 1/2 lb ground beef
- 1/2 onion, chopped
- 2 garlic cloves, minced
- 1 can (14 oz) diced tomatoes
- 1/2 cup tomato sauce
- 1 tsp dried oregano
- Salt and pepper, to taste
- 4 oz lasagna noodles, uncooked
- 1 cup ricotta cheese
- 1 cup shredded mozzarella cheese
- 1/4 cup grated Parmesan cheese
- Fresh parsley, chopped, for serving (optional)

Instructions:
1. Heat a large skillet over medium-high heat. Add the ground beef, chopped onion, and minced garlic. Cook, stirring occasionally, until the beef is browned and the onion is softened, about 5-7 minutes.
2. Add the diced tomatoes, tomato sauce, dried oregano, salt, and pepper to the skillet with the beef mixture. Stir everything together and bring the sauce to a simmer.
3. Spread a thin layer of the meat sauce on the bottom of the slow cooker. Break the lasagna noodles into pieces to fit in a single layer over the sauce. Top the noodles with a layer of the ricotta cheese, followed by a layer of the shredded mozzarella cheese. Repeat the layers, ending with a layer of the meat sauce. Sprinkle the grated Parmesan cheese on top.
4. Cover the slow cooker and cook on low for 4-6 hours or on high for 2-3 hours, until the lasagna noodles are cooked through and the cheese is melted and bubbly.
5. Let the lasagna rest for about 10 minutes before serving. Sprinkle fresh chopped parsley on top, if desired.

BEEF

Beef and Broccoli

Tender beef and broccoli cooked in a savory sauce. Serve with rice.

Food Preparation: 10-15min | Cook Time: 3-6 hours | Yield: 2 servings

Ingredients:
- 1/2 lb flank steak, thinly sliced against the grain
- 2 cups broccoli florets
- 1/2 onion, sliced
- 2 garlic cloves, minced
- 1/4 cup soy sauce
- 2 tbsp brown sugar
- 2 tbsp cornstarch
- 1 tsp sesame oil
- 1/2 tsp ground ginger
- 1/4 tsp red pepper flakes
- Salt and pepper, to taste
- Cooked rice, for serving

Instructions:
1. Add the thinly sliced flank steak, broccoli florets, sliced onion, and minced garlic to the slow cooker.
2. In a small bowl, whisk together the soy sauce, brown sugar, cornstarch, sesame oil, ground ginger, red pepper flakes, salt, and pepper until smooth. Pour the sauce over the beef and broccoli in the slow cooker. Stir everything together.
3. Cover the slow cooker and cook on low for 4-6 hours or high for 2-3 hours, until the beef is tender and the broccoli is cooked through.
4. Serve the Beef and Broccoli hot, over cooked rice.

Slow Cooker Beef Stroganoff

Tender chunks of beef in a rich and creamy sauce served over egg noodles.

Food Preparation: 15-20min | Cook Time: 4-8 hours | Yield: 2 servings

Ingredients:
- 1/2 lb beef sirloin, cut into thin strips
- 1/2 onion, chopped
- 1 garlic clove, minced
- 4 oz sliced mushrooms
- 1/2 can (5 oz) cream of mushroom soup
- 1/2 cup beef broth
- 1/2 tbsp Worcestershire sauce
- 1/2 tsp Dijon mustard
- 1/4 tsp paprika
- 1/8 tsp salt
- 1/8 tsp black pepper
- 1/4 cup sour cream
- 4 oz egg noodles, cooked according to package instructions

Instructions:
1. In a large skillet, cook the beef over medium-high heat until browned on all sides, then transfer to a slow cooker.
2. In the same skillet, sauté the onion, garlic, and mushrooms until softened, then add to the slow cooker.
3. In a separate bowl, whisk together the cream of mushroom soup, beef broth, Worcestershire sauce, Dijon mustard, paprika, salt, and pepper.
4. Pour the soup mixture into the slow cooker and stir to combine with the beef and veggies.
5. Cover and cook on low for 6-8 hours or on high for 3-4 hours.
6. About 30 minutes before serving, stir in the sour cream.
7. Serve the stroganoff over the cooked egg noodles.

BEEF

Slow Cooker Korean Beef Tacos

Delicious and flavorful fusion of Korean and Mexican cuisine.

Food Preparation: 15-20min | Cook Time: 6-8 hours | Yield: 2 servings

Ingredients:
- 1 pound beef chuck roast, trimmed and cut into bite-sized pieces
- 1/2 cup soy sauce
- 1/4 cup brown sugar
- 2 tablespoons sesame oil
- 2 tablespoons rice vinegar
- 1 tablespoon gochujang (Korean chili paste)
- 1 tablespoon grated fresh ginger
- 2 garlic cloves, minced
- 1/2 onion, sliced
- Flour or corn tortillas
- Optional toppings: shredded lettuce, sliced radishes, chopped cilantro, lime wedges

Instructions:
1. In a bowl, whisk together soy sauce, brown sugar, sesame oil, rice vinegar, gochujang, ginger, and garlic.
2. Add beef and onion to the slow cooker. Pour the sauce over the beef and stir to coat.
3. Cook on low for 6-8 hours.
4. Serve with tortillas and desired toppings

Slow Cooker Beef and Guinness Stew

The beef is cooked low and slow in a rich and flavorful broth made with Guinness beer, beef broth, and a variety of vegetables and herbs.

Food Preparation: 15-20min | Cook Time: 6-8 hours | Yield: 2 servings

Ingredients:
- 1 pound beef chuck roast, trimmed and cut into bite-sized pieces
- 1/4 cup all-purpose flour
- 1 teaspoon salt
- 1/2 teaspoon black pepper
- 2 tablespoons olive oil
- 1 onion, chopped
- 2 garlic cloves, minced
- 2 carrots, chopped
- 2 celery stalks, chopped
- 1 can (14.9 oz) Guinness beer
- 1 cup beef broth
- 2 bay leaves
- 1 tablespoon tomato paste
- 1 tablespoon Worcestershire sauce

Instructions:
1. In a large bowl, combine flour, salt, and pepper. Dredge the beef in the flour mixture.
2. Heat olive oil in a large skillet over medium-high heat. Add the beef and cook until browned on all sides, about 5-7 minutes.
3. Transfer the beef to the slow cooker. Add onion, garlic, carrots, and celery.
4. In a small bowl, whisk together Guinness beer, beef broth, tomato paste, Worcestershire sauce, and bay leaves. Pour the mixture over the beef and vegetables.
5. Cook on low for 6-8 hours.
6. Discard the bay leaves and serve hot.

BEEF

Slow Cooker Beef Gyros

This dish features tender, seasoned beef with all the classic gyro toppings.

Food Preparation: 10-15min | Cook Time: 6-8 hours | Yield: 2 servings

Ingredients:
- 1 lb beef stew meat
- 2 garlic cloves (minced)
- 1 tsp dried oregano
- 1 tsp dried basil
- 1/2 tsp onion powder
- 1/4 tsp salt
- 1/4 tsp black pepper
- 1 tbsp lemon juice
- 2 pita breads
- tzatziki sauce
- sliced tomatoes
- sliced red onion

Instructions:
1. In a small bowl, mix together garlic, oregano, basil, onion powder, salt, and black pepper.
2. Place beef in slow cooker and sprinkle spice mixture over beef.
3. Add lemon juice and stir to combine.
4. Cover and cook on low for 6-8 hours or until beef is tender.
5. Serve beef in pita breads with tzatziki sauce, tomatoes, and red onion.

Slow Cooker Spicy Chicken and Lentil Soup

A hearty and spicy soup packed with protein from lentils and chicken, perfect for a filling and warming meal.

Food Preparation: 10-15min | Cook Time: 6-8 hours | Yield: 2 servings

Ingredients:
- 1 boneless, skinless chicken breast, cut into small pieces
- 1/2 cup dried lentils, rinsed and drained
- 2 cups low-sodium chicken broth
- 1 can (14.5 oz) diced tomatoes, undrained
- 1/2 cup diced onion
- 1/2 cup diced carrot
- 1/2 cup diced celery
- 2 cloves garlic, minced
- 1 tsp. cumin
- 1 tsp. chili powder
- 1/2 tsp. paprika
- 1/4 tsp. cayenne pepper (or more, to taste)
- Salt and pepper, to taste
- 1 tbsp. chopped fresh cilantro

Instructions:
1. Add chicken, lentils, chicken broth, diced tomatoes, onion, carrot, celery, garlic, cumin, chili powder, paprika, cayenne pepper, salt, and pepper to a 2-quart slow cooker. Stir to combine.
2. Cover and cook on low for 6-8 hours, or until lentils are tender.
3. Stir in chopped cilantro before serving.

SOUP

Slow Cooker Split Pea Soup

A classic and hearty soup made with split peas, carrots, onions, and ham or bacon, perfect for a cozy and filling meal.

Food Preparation: 10-15min | Cook Time: 6-10 hours | Yield: 2 servings

Ingredients:
- 1/2 pound dried green split peas
- 2 cups vegetable broth
- 2 cups water
- 1/2 onion, diced
- 1 carrot, diced
- 1 celery stalk, diced
- 1 garlic clove, minced
- 1/2 teaspoon dried thyme
- 1 bay leaf
- Salt and pepper to taste
- Optional: cooked ham, chopped (about 1/2 cup)

Instructions:
1. Rinse the split peas and pick out any debris.
2. In a slow cooker, combine the split peas, vegetable broth, water, onion, carrot, celery, garlic, thyme, bay leaf, and a pinch of salt and pepper.
3. Cover and cook on high for 4-6 hours or on low for 8-10 hours.
4. If using ham, add it during the last hour of cooking.
5. Remove the bay leaf and discard.
6. Use an immersion blender to blend the soup until smooth, or transfer the soup to a blender and blend in batches.
7. Adjust seasoning with salt and pepper as needed.
8. Serve hot with crusty bread, if desired.

Slow Cooker Italian Wedding Soup

A classic Italian soup made with meatballs, pasta, vegetables, and a flavorful broth, perfect for a comforting and satisfying meal.

Food Preparation: 15-20min | Cook Time: 4-8 hours | Yield: 2 servings

Ingredients:
- 2 cups chicken broth
- 1/2 cup uncooked orzo pasta
- 1/2 pound ground turkey
- 1/4 cup breadcrumbs
- 1/4 cup grated parmesan cheese
- 1 egg
- 1/2 teaspoon dried basil
- 1/2 teaspoon dried oregano
- 1/4 teaspoon salt
- 1/4 teaspoon black pepper
- 1 cup chopped fresh spinach
- 1/4 cup chopped fresh parsley
- 1/4 cup chopped onion
- 1/4 cup chopped carrots
- 1/4 cup chopped celery

Instructions:
1. In a large mixing bowl, combine the ground turkey, breadcrumbs, parmesan cheese, egg, basil, oregano, salt, and black pepper. Mix well to combine and form into small meatballs.
2. Add the chicken broth, orzo pasta, meatballs, onion, carrots, and celery to the slow cooker. Stir to combine.
3. Cover and cook on low for 6-8 hours, or on high for 3-4 hours, until the meatballs are cooked through and the vegetables are tender.
4. Stir in the chopped spinach and parsley and cook for an additional 5-10 minutes, until the spinach is wilted.
5. Serve hot and enjoy!

Note: You can also add in some additional vegetables such as zucchini, bell peppers, or mushrooms if desired.

SOUP

Slow Cooker Chicken and Wild Rice Soup

A comforting and creamy soup made with chicken, wild rice, and veggies.

Food Preparation: 10-15min | Cook Time: 6-7 hours | Yield: 2 servings

Ingredients:
- 1/2 cup wild rice
- 1 tablespoon olive oil
- 1 small onion, chopped
- 2 cloves garlic, minced
- 2 cups chicken broth
- 1 cup water
- 1 boneless, skinless chicken breast, cut into bite-size pieces
- 1 teaspoon dried thyme
- 1/2 teaspoon dried rosemary
- 1/2 teaspoon salt
- 1/4 teaspoon black pepper
- 1 cup chopped vegetables (such as carrots, celery, and mushrooms)
- 1/2 cup milk or cream

Instructions:
1. Rinse the wild rice in a fine-mesh strainer and set aside.
2. In a large skillet, heat the olive oil over medium heat. Add the chopped onion and sauté for 3-4 minutes, or until the onion is soft and translucent. Add the minced garlic and sauté for an additional 30 seconds.
3. Transfer the onion and garlic mixture to the slow cooker. Add the chicken broth, water, chicken, wild rice, thyme, rosemary, salt, and black pepper to the slow cooker and stir to combine.
4. Cover and cook on low for 6-7 hours, or until the chicken is cooked through and the rice is tender.
5. Stir in the chopped vegetables and milk or cream. Cover and cook on low for an additional 30 minutes, or until the vegetables are tender and the soup is hot.
6. Serve hot, garnished with fresh parsley or croutons if desired.

Slow Cooker Ham and White Bean Soup

SOUP

A classic ham and bean soup made with tender ham, white beans, carrots, and celery, perfect for a cozy meal on a chilly day.

Food Preparation: 15-20min | Cook Time: 4-8 hours | Yield: 2 servings

Ingredients:
- 1/2 lb. ham, diced
- 1/2 onion, diced
- 2 cloves garlic, minced
- 2 cups chicken or vegetable broth
- 1 can (15 oz.) white beans, drained and rinsed
- 1/2 tsp. dried thyme
- 1/4 tsp. black pepper
- 1 bay leaf
- 1 cup chopped kale or spinach (optional)

Instructions:
1. In a slow cooker, combine the diced ham, onion, garlic, broth, white beans, thyme, black pepper, and bay leaf. Stir to combine.
2. Cover and cook on low for 6-8 hours or on high for 3-4 hours.
3. About 30 minutes before serving, add the chopped kale or spinach to the slow cooker and stir. Cover and continue cooking until the greens are wilted and tender.
4. Remove the bay leaf and serve hot.

SOUP

Slow Cooker Beef and Barley Soup

A hearty and nutritious soup made with beef, barley, and veggies.

Food Preparation: 15-20min | Cook Time: 6-8 hours | Yield: 2 servings

Ingredients:
- 1/2 pound beef chuck roast, cut into small cubes
- 1/2 cup pearl barley
- 2 cups beef broth
- 1 onion, chopped
- 2 carrots, chopped
- 2 celery stalks, chopped
- 1 bay leaf
- 1 tsp dried thyme
- Salt and pepper, to taste

Instructions:
1. Add the beef, barley, beef broth, onion, carrots, celery, bay leaf, thyme, salt, and pepper to the slow cooker.
2. Stir everything together to combine.
3. Cover the slow cooker and cook on low for 6-8 hours, or until the beef and vegetables are tender.
4. Taste and adjust seasoning as needed.
5. Serve hot with crusty bread or crackers.

Note: You can also add other vegetables, such as potatoes or mushrooms, to this soup if desired.

SOUP

Slow Cooker Spicy Black Bean Soup

A hearty and spicy soup made with black beans, veggies, and a blend of spices. Serve with some crusty bread for a complete meal.

Food Preparation: 10-15min | Cook Time: 4-8 hours | Yield: 2 servings

Ingredients:
- 1 can (15 oz) black beans, drained and rinsed
- 1/2 cup salsa
- 1/2 cup chicken or vegetable broth
- 1/4 cup chopped onion
- 1/4 cup chopped red bell pepper
- 1 garlic clove, minced
- 1/2 tsp ground cumin
- 1/2 tsp chili powder
- Salt and pepper, to taste
- 1 tbsp lime juice
- Optional toppings: sour cream, chopped cilantro, diced avocado, shredded cheese

Instructions:
1. In a small slow cooker, combine the black beans, salsa, chicken or vegetable broth, chopped onion, chopped red bell pepper, minced garlic, ground cumin, chili powder, salt, and pepper.
2. Stir to combine and cook on low for 6-8 hours or on high for 3-4 hours, until the vegetables are tender and the flavors are well combined.
3. Stir in the lime juice and season with additional salt and pepper, if needed.
4. Ladle the soup into bowls and top with desired toppings, such as sour cream, chopped cilantro, diced avocado, and shredded cheese.

SOUP

Lentil Soup

A comforting and healthy soup made with lentils, vegetables and spices. Serve with crusty bread.

Food Preparation: 10-15min | Cook Time: 6-10 hours | Yield: 2 servings

Ingredients:
- 1 cup dried green or brown lentils, rinsed and drained
- 1 onion, chopped
- 2 garlic cloves, minced
- 2 medium carrots, chopped
- 2 celery stalks, chopped
- 4 cups vegetable or chicken broth
- 1 can (14 oz) diced tomatoes
- 1 tbsp olive oil
- 1 tsp dried thyme
- Salt and pepper, to taste
- Lemon wedges and fresh parsley, for serving (optional)

Instructions:
1. Add the rinsed lentils, chopped onion, minced garlic, chopped carrots, chopped celery, vegetable or chicken broth, diced tomatoes, olive oil, dried thyme, salt, and pepper to the slow cooker. Stir everything together.
2. Cover the slow cooker and cook on high for 4-6 hours or on low for 8-10 hours, until the lentils are tender and the soup is thickened.
3. Taste the soup and adjust the seasoning as needed.
4. Serve the Lentil Soup hot, garnished with lemon wedges and fresh parsley, if desired.

Slow Cooker Tomato Basil Soup

SOUP

A classic and comforting soup made with fresh tomatoes and basil, perfect for dipping grilled cheese sandwiches.

Food Preparation: 10-15min | Cook Time: 4-8 hours | Yield: 2 servings

Ingredients:
- 1 can (14.5 oz) diced tomatoes, undrained
- 1/2 cup vegetable broth
- 1/4 cup chopped onion
- 2 garlic cloves, minced
- 1/2 tsp dried basil
- Salt and pepper, to taste
- 1/4 cup heavy cream (optional)

Instructions:
1. Add the diced tomatoes (undrained), vegetable broth, chopped onion, minced garlic, dried basil, salt, and pepper to a small slow cooker.
2. Cover and cook on low for 6-8 hours or on high for 3-4 hours, until the vegetables are tender and the flavors have melded together.
3. Use an immersion blender or transfer the soup to a blender and puree until smooth.
4. If desired, stir in the heavy cream to make the soup creamy.
5. Serve hot and enjoy your Slow Cooker Tomato Basil Soup for 2!

Note: You can also add a splash of balsamic vinegar or a sprinkle of grated Parmesan cheese for extra flavor.

SOUP

Slow Cooker Minestrone Soup

A classic and hearty Italian soup made with veggies, beans, and pasta.

Food Preparation: 15-20min | Cook Time: 4-8 hours | Yield: 2 servings

Ingredients:
- 1/2 onion, chopped
- 2 cloves garlic, minced
- 1 medium carrot, chopped
- 1 small zucchini, chopped
- 1 cup chopped fresh spinach
- 1 can (14.5 oz) diced tomatoes, undrained
- 1 can (15 oz) kidney beans, drained and rinsed
- 2 cups vegetable broth
- 1 tsp dried basil
- 1 tsp dried oregano
- 1/2 cup small pasta (such as ditalini or elbow macaroni)
- Salt and pepper, to taste
- Shredded Parmesan cheese, for serving (optional)

Instructions:
1. In a slow cooker, combine the chopped onion, minced garlic, chopped carrot, chopped zucchini, chopped spinach, diced tomatoes, kidney beans, vegetable broth, dried basil, and dried oregano.
2. Cover and cook on low heat for 6-8 hours, or on high heat for 3-4 hours.
3. About 30 minutes before serving, stir in the small pasta and continue cooking until the pasta is tender.
4. Season with salt and pepper, to taste.
5. Serve hot, topped with shredded Parmesan cheese, if desired. Enjoy!

Vegetable Curry

A delicious vegetarian curry made with a variety of vegetables, chickpeas and spices. Serve with rice.

Food Preparation: 25-30min | Cook Time: 3-6 hours | Yield: 2 servings

Ingredients:
- 1 tbsp vegetable oil
- 1 small onion, chopped
- 1 garlic clove, minced
- 1 tbsp curry powder
- 1/2 tsp ground cumin
- 1/2 tsp ground coriander
- 1/2 tsp turmeric
- 1/2 tsp paprika
- 1/4 tsp cayenne pepper (optional)
- 1/2 cup vegetable broth
- 1/2 cup coconut milk
- 1 small sweet potato, peeled and chopped
- 1 small zucchini, chopped
- 1/2 cup green beans, trimmed
- 1/2 cup frozen peas
- Salt and pepper, to taste
- Fresh cilantro, chopped (optional)

Instructions:
1. Heat the vegetable oil in a large skillet over medium heat. Add the onion and garlic and cook until the onion is soft and translucent, about 5 minutes.
2. Add the curry powder, cumin, coriander, turmeric, paprika, and cayenne pepper (if using) and stir to coat the onion and garlic in the spices. Cook for an additional 2-3 minutes.
3. Transfer the onion and spice mixture to a slow cooker.
4. Add the vegetable broth, coconut milk, sweet potato, zucchini, and green beans to the slow cooker. Stir everything together.
5. Cover the slow cooker and cook on low for 4-6 hours or high for 2-3 hours, until the vegetables are tender.
6. Add the frozen peas to the slow cooker and stir everything together. Cook for an additional 15-20 minutes, until the peas are heated through.
7. Season the vegetable curry with salt and pepper, to taste.
8. Serve the vegetable curry hot, garnished with fresh cilantro (if desired) and with rice or naan bread on the side.

VEGE

Slow Cooker Lentil and Vegetable Stew

A hearty and nutritious vegetarian stew made with lentils, veggies, and a blend of spices.

Food Preparation: 15-20min | Cook Time: 4-8 hours | Yield: 2 servings

Ingredients:
- 1 cup dried green lentils, rinsed and drained
- 2 cups vegetable broth
- 1 onion, chopped
- 2 cloves garlic, minced
- 2 carrots, chopped
- 2 celery stalks, chopped
- 1 sweet potato, peeled and diced
- 1 can diced tomatoes (14.5 oz)
- 1 tsp ground cumin
- 1 tsp smoked paprika
- 1/2 tsp ground coriander
- Salt and pepper, to taste
- 2 tbsp chopped fresh parsley

Instructions:
1. In a slow cooker, add the lentils, vegetable broth, onion, garlic, carrots, celery, sweet potato, diced tomatoes, cumin, smoked paprika, coriander, salt, and pepper.
2. Stir well to combine.
3. Cook on low for 8 hours or high for 4 hours, or until the lentils and vegetables are tender.
4. Serve hot with chopped fresh parsley on top.

VEGE

Slow Cooker Moroccan Vegetable Stew

A hearty and flavorful vegetarian stew with chickpeas, sweet potatoes, and a blend of Moroccan spices.

Food Preparation: 10-15min | Cook Time: 4-8 hours | Yield: 2 servings

Ingredients:
- 1 tbsp olive oil
- 1/2 onion, chopped
- 1 garlic clove, minced
- 1 carrot, peeled and chopped
- 1 sweet potato, peeled and chopped
- 1/2 red bell pepper, chopped
- 1/2 tsp ground cumin
- 1/2 tsp ground coriander
- 1/4 tsp ground cinnamon
- 1/4 tsp ground ginger
- 1/4 tsp paprika
- 1/8 tsp cayenne pepper (optional)
- 1/2 can (14 oz) diced tomatoes, with juice
- 1/2 can (14 oz) chickpeas, drained and rinsed
- 1/2 cup vegetable broth
- Salt and pepper, to taste
- Fresh cilantro, chopped (optional)
- Cooked couscous, for serving

Instructions:
1. Heat the olive oil in a large skillet over medium heat. Add the onion and garlic and sauté for 2-3 minutes until softened.
2. Add the carrot, sweet potato, and red bell pepper and sauté for another 2-3 minutes.
3. Add the cumin, coriander, cinnamon, ginger, paprika, and cayenne pepper (if using) and stir to combine.
4. Add the diced tomatoes, chickpeas, and vegetable broth to the slow cooker. Stir in the sautéed vegetables and season with salt and pepper to taste.
5. Cover and cook on low for 6-8 hours or on high for 3-4 hours, until the vegetables are tender.
6. Serve over cooked couscous and sprinkle with fresh cilantro (if desired).

VEGE

Slow Cooker Ratatouille

A flavorful and colorful vegetable stew made with eggplant, zucchini, bell peppers, and tomatoes.

Food Preparation: 15-20min | Cook Time: 4-8 hours | Yield: 2 servings

Ingredients:
- 1 medium zucchini, sliced
- 1 medium yellow squash, sliced
- 1 small eggplant, diced
- 1 red bell pepper, diced
- 1 small onion, diced
- 1 can (14.5 oz) diced tomatoes, undrained
- 2 garlic cloves, minced
- 1 tsp dried basil
- 1 tsp dried oregano
- Salt and pepper, to taste
- 1/4 cup chopped fresh parsley (optional)

Instructions:
1. Add the sliced zucchini, sliced yellow squash, diced eggplant, diced red bell pepper, diced onion, undrained diced tomatoes, minced garlic, dried basil, dried oregano, salt, and pepper to a small slow cooker.
2. Stir to combine all the ingredients.
3. Cover and cook on low for 6-8 hours or on high for 3-4 hours, until the vegetables are tender and cooked through.
4. Stir in the chopped fresh parsley (optional).
5. Serve hot and enjoy your Slow Cooker Ratatouille for 2!

Note: You can also add a splash of balsamic vinegar or a sprinkle of grated Parmesan cheese for extra flavor. Ratatouille goes well with crusty bread or over pasta.

VEGE

Slow Cooker Sweet Potato and Black Bean Chili

A flavorful and hearty vegetarian chili made with sweet potatoes, black beans, and a blend of spices.

Food Preparation: 10-15min | Cook Time: 4-8 hours | Yield: 2 servings

Ingredients:
- 1 large sweet potato, peeled and chopped
- 1 can black beans, drained and rinsed
- 1 can diced tomatoes
- 1 small onion, diced
- 2 cloves garlic, minced
- 1 tsp chili powder
- 1/2 tsp cumin
- 1/2 tsp paprika
- 1/4 tsp cinnamon
- 1/4 tsp salt
- 1/4 tsp black pepper
- 1 cup vegetable broth
- 1 tbsp olive oil
- 2 tbsp chopped fresh cilantro (optional)

Instructions:
1. Heat the olive oil in a skillet over medium heat. Add the onion and garlic and sauté until softened, about 5 minutes.
2. Transfer the onion and garlic to the slow cooker. Add the sweet potato, black beans, diced tomatoes, chili powder, cumin, paprika, cinnamon, salt, black pepper, and vegetable broth.
3. Stir everything together until well combined.
4. Cover and cook on low for 6-8 hours, or on high for 3-4 hours, until the sweet potatoes are tender.
5. Serve hot, garnished with fresh cilantro if desired.

VEGE

Slow Cooker Vegetarian Chili

A flavorful and hearty vegetarian chili made with beans, veggies, and a blend of spices.

Food Preparation: 15-20min | Cook Time: 4-8 hours | Yield: 2 servings

Ingredients:
- 1 can (15 oz) black beans, drained and rinsed
- 1 can (15 oz) kidney beans, drained and rinsed
- 1 can (14.5 oz) diced tomatoes, undrained
- 1 green bell pepper, diced
- 1 small onion, diced
- 1 clove garlic, minced
- 1 tbsp chili powder
- 1 tsp ground cumin
- 1/2 tsp paprika
- 1/2 tsp salt
- 1/4 tsp black pepper
- 1 cup vegetable broth
- 1/4 cup uncooked quinoa
- 1/2 cup frozen corn kernels
- 1 tbsp olive oil

Instructions:
1. In a large slow cooker, combine the black beans, kidney beans, diced tomatoes, green bell pepper, onion, garlic, chili powder, cumin, paprika, salt, and black pepper.
2. Add the vegetable broth and quinoa to the slow cooker and stir to combine.
3. Cover and cook on low for 6-8 hours, or on high for 3-4 hours, until the vegetables are tender and the quinoa is cooked.
4. About 30 minutes before serving, stir in the frozen corn kernels and olive oil.
5. Serve the chili hot, garnished with your favorite toppings such as shredded cheese, chopped cilantro, or diced avocado.

Slow Cooker Vegetarian Lasagna

VEGE

A delicious and cheesy lasagna made with layers of veggies and cheese.

Food Preparation: 25-30min | Cook Time: 4-5 hours | Yield: 2 servings

Ingredients:
- 4 lasagna noodles, uncooked
- 1/2 cup chopped onion
- 1/2 cup chopped red bell pepper
- 1 clove garlic, minced
- 1 cup sliced mushrooms
- 1 can (14.5 oz) diced tomatoes
- 1 can (8 oz) tomato sauce
- 1/2 cup water
- 1 tsp dried basil
- 1 tsp dried oregano
- 1/4 tsp salt
- 1/4 tsp black pepper
- 1 cup ricotta cheese
- 1 cup shredded mozzarella cheese
- 1/4 cup grated Parmesan cheese

Instructions:
1. In a large skillet, cook the onion, red bell pepper, garlic, and mushrooms over medium heat until the vegetables are tender.
2. Stir in the diced tomatoes, tomato sauce, water, basil, oregano, salt, and pepper.
3. In a small bowl, mix together the ricotta cheese, mozzarella cheese, and Parmesan cheese.
4. In a 2-quart slow cooker, spread a thin layer of the tomato sauce mixture on the bottom of the pot.
5. Break 2 lasagna noodles into pieces and arrange them over the tomato sauce.
6. Spoon 1/3 of the cheese mixture over the lasagna noodles.
7. Repeat layers, ending with the cheese mixture on top.
8. Pour the remaining tomato sauce mixture over the top.
9. Cover and cook on low for 4-5 hours.
10. Let the lasagna cool for a few minutes before serving.

Note: You can add any additional vegetables, such as spinach, zucchini, or eggplant, to the recipe as well.

VEGE

Slow Cooker Ratatouille with Chickpeas

A vegetarian version of the French classic dish, ratatouille, made with chickpeas for added protein and served over rice or quinoa.

Food Preparation: 15-20min | Cook Time: 4-8 hours | Yield: 2 servings

Ingredients:
- 1 eggplant, diced
- 1 zucchini, diced
- 1 yellow squash, diced
- 1 red bell pepper, diced
- 1 onion, diced
- 2 cloves garlic, minced
- 1 can chickpeas, drained and rinsed
- 1 can crushed tomatoes
- 1 teaspoon dried basil
- 1 teaspoon dried oregano
- Salt and pepper, to taste

Instructions:
1. Add the diced eggplant, zucchini, yellow squash, red bell pepper, onion, garlic, and chickpeas to the slow cooker.
2. Pour in the can of crushed tomatoes and stir to combine.
3. Add the dried basil and oregano, and season with salt and pepper to taste.
4. Cover the slow cooker and cook on low for 6-8 hours or on high for 3-4 hours.
5. Serve hot, garnished with fresh basil or parsley if desired.

Slow Cooker Cheesy Broccoli and Rice Casserole

comforting and cheesy rice casserole packed with broccoli, perfect as a side dish or a vegetarian main course.

Food Preparation: 10-15min | Cook Time: 2-3 hours | Yield: 2 servings

Ingredients:
- 1 cup broccoli florets, chopped
- 1/2 cup uncooked white rice
- 1/2 cup shredded cheddar cheese
- 1/2 cup milk
- 1/2 cup chicken broth
- 1/4 teaspoon garlic powder
- Salt and pepper, to taste

Instructions:
1. Spray the slow cooker with cooking spray.
2. Add broccoli florets and uncooked white rice to the slow cooker.
3. In a separate bowl, mix together the shredded cheddar cheese, milk, chicken broth, garlic powder, salt, and pepper.
4. Pour the cheese mixture over the broccoli and rice in the slow cooker, and stir everything together.
5. Cover the slow cooker and cook on low for 2-3 hours, or until the rice is cooked and the broccoli is tender.
6. Once the casserole is cooked, give it a good stir to combine everything together, and serve hot.

VEGE

PORK

Slow Cooker Balsamic Pork Tenderloin

Pork tenderloin cooked in a sweet and tangy balsamic glaze with garlic and herbs, served over rice or roasted vegetables.

Food Preparation: 10-15min | Cook Time: 4-6 hours | Yield: 2 servings

Ingredients:
- 1 lb pork tenderloin
- 1/2 cup balsamic vinegar
- 1/4 cup honey
- 1/4 cup low-sodium soy sauce
- 2 garlic cloves, minced
- 1 tsp dried oregano
- 1/2 tsp dried basil
- 1/4 tsp red pepper flakes
- Salt and pepper, to taste

Instructions:
1. In a bowl, mix together balsamic vinegar, honey, soy sauce, garlic, oregano, basil, red pepper flakes, salt, and pepper.
2. Place the pork tenderloin in the slow cooker.
3. Pour the balsamic mixture over the pork, making sure to coat it evenly.
4. Cover and cook on low for 4-6 hours, or until the pork is cooked through and tender.
5. Remove the pork from the slow cooker and let it rest for 5-10 minutes before slicing.
6. Serve the pork with the remaining sauce from the slow cooker.

Slow Cooker Sweet and Sour Pork

Juicy pork in a tangy and sweet sauce with peppers and onions, served over rice or noodles.

Food Preparation: 10-15min | Cook Time: 4-8 hours | Yield: 2 servings

Ingredients:
- 1 pound pork tenderloin, cut into bite-sized pieces
- 1/2 cup chopped onion
- 1/2 cup chopped green bell pepper
- 1/2 cup chopped pineapple (fresh or canned)
- 1/4 cup ketchup
- 1/4 cup apple cider vinegar
- 2 tablespoons brown sugar
- 1 tablespoon soy sauce
- 1/2 teaspoon garlic powder
- 1/2 teaspoon ginger powder
- 2 tablespoons cornstarch
- 2 tablespoons cold water
- Cooked rice, for serving

Instructions:
1. In a 4-quart slow cooker, add the pork, onion, bell pepper, and pineapple.
2. In a small bowl, whisk together the ketchup, apple cider vinegar, brown sugar, soy sauce, garlic powder, and ginger powder.
3. Pour the sauce over the pork and vegetables in the slow cooker and stir to combine.
4. Cover the slow cooker and cook on low for 6-8 hours or on high for 3-4 hours, until the pork is cooked through and tender.
5. In a small bowl, whisk together the cornstarch and cold water to make a slurry.
6. Stir the slurry into the slow cooker and cook on high for an additional 30 minutes, until the sauce has thickened.
7. Serve the sweet and sour pork over cooked rice.

PORK

Slow Cooker Pulled Pork

Tender pork slow-cooked with barbecue sauce. Serve with coleslaw and buns.

Food Preparation: 10-15min | Cook Time: 6-10 hours | Yield: 2 servings

Ingredients:
- 1 pound boneless pork shoulder or pork butt
- 1/2 onion, diced
- 2 cloves garlic, minced
- 1/2 cup chicken broth
- 1/2 cup barbecue sauce
- 1 tbsp brown sugar
- 1 tsp smoked paprika
- 1/2 tsp salt
- 1/4 tsp black pepper

Instructions:
1. Place the pork shoulder or pork butt in the slow cooker.
2. In a separate bowl, whisk together the onion, garlic, chicken broth, barbecue sauce, brown sugar, smoked paprika, salt, and black pepper. Pour the mixture over the pork in the slow cooker.
3. Cover the slow cooker and cook on low for 8-10 hours or high for 4-6 hours, until the pork is tender and falls apart easily with a fork.
4. Remove the pork from the slow cooker and shred it with two forks.
5. Return the shredded pork to the slow cooker and stir it into the sauce.
6. Cover the slow cooker and cook on low for an additional 30 minutes to let the pork absorb more of the sauce.
7. Serve the pulled pork hot on a sandwich roll or hamburger bun, with additional barbecue sauce and coleslaw, if desired.

Slow Cooker Pork Carnitas

PORK

The pork is tender and juicy, with a crispy exterior, and is seasoned with a blend of spices that make it mouth-watering and flavorful. Serve it with your favorite toppings for a delicious and satisfying meal.

Food Preparation: 15-20min | Cook Time: 6-8 hours | Yield: 2 servings

Ingredients:
- 1 lb pork shoulder, trimmed and cut into 2-inch pieces
- 1 tablespoon olive oil
- 1 teaspoon salt
- 1/2 teaspoon black pepper
- 1 teaspoon ground cumin
- 1 teaspoon dried oregano
- 1/2 teaspoon smoked paprika
- 1/2 teaspoon garlic powder
- 1/2 teaspoon onion powder
- 1/4 teaspoon cayenne pepper
- 1/4 cup chicken broth
- 1 lime, juiced

Instructions:
1. In a small bowl, mix together the salt, black pepper, cumin, oregano, smoked paprika, garlic powder, onion powder, and cayenne pepper.
2. Rub the spice mixture all over the pork shoulder pieces.
3. Heat the olive oil in a large skillet over medium-high heat. Brown the pork pieces on all sides, about 3-4 minutes per side.
4. Transfer the pork to a slow cooker and pour in the chicken broth.
5. Cover and cook on low for 6-8 hours, until the pork is tender and can be easily shredded.
6. Once the pork is cooked, remove it from the slow cooker and shred it with two forks.
7. Strain the liquid from the slow cooker and return the shredded pork to the slow cooker.
8. Pour the lime juice over the pork and stir to combine.
9. Turn the slow cooker to high and cook for an additional 30 minutes, until the pork is crispy and caramelized.
10. Serve the Slow Cooker Pork Carnitas with your favorite toppings, such as diced onion, chopped cilantro, sliced jalapeños, and shredded cheese.

PORK

Slow Cooker Pork and Bean Chili

Made with tender pork, kidney beans, and aromatic spices, it's a dish that's sure to warm you up from the inside out.

Food Preparation: 10-15min | Cook Time: 6-8 hours | Yield: 2 servings

Ingredients:
- 1/2 lb pork shoulder, trimmed and cut into small cubes
- 1 can kidney beans, drained and rinsed
- 1/2 onion, chopped
- 1 garlic clove, minced
- 1 tablespoon chili powder
- 1 teaspoon cumin
- 1/2 teaspoon smoked paprika
- 1/2 teaspoon oregano
- 1/2 teaspoon salt
- 1/4 teaspoon black pepper
- 1 can diced tomatoes
- 1 cup chicken or vegetable broth
- Optional toppings: shredded cheese, chopped cilantro, sour cream

Instructions:
1. Heat a skillet over medium-high heat and brown the pork cubes on all sides.
2. Transfer the pork to a slow cooker and add the kidney beans, onion, garlic, chili powder, cumin, smoked paprika, oregano, salt, black pepper, diced tomatoes, and chicken or vegetable broth. Stir well to combine.
3. Cover the slow cooker and cook on low heat for 6-8 hours, or until the pork is tender and the chili is thick and flavorful.
4. Serve the chili hot with your favorite toppings, if desired.
5. Food Preparation: Trim and cut pork into small cubes, chop onions and mince garlic.
6. Cook Time: 6-8 hours on low heat.

Slow Cooker Cuban Mojo Pork

Tender and flavorful pork with a tangy and citrusy Cuban mojo marinade.

Food Preparation: 15-20min | Cook Time: 6-8 hours | Yield: 2 servings

Ingredients:
- 1 lb. pork shoulder, cut into 2-inch pieces
- 1/4 cup orange juice
- 1/4 cup lime juice
- 4 cloves garlic, minced
- 2 teaspoons ground cumin
- 1 teaspoon dried oregano
- 1/4 cup olive oil
- Salt and pepper to taste

Instructions:
1. In a small bowl, mix together the orange juice, lime juice, garlic, cumin, oregano, olive oil, salt, and pepper.
2. Place the pork pieces in the slow cooker and pour the mojo marinade over the top, making sure each piece is coated.
3. Cover and cook on low for 6-8 hours, or until the pork is cooked through and tender.
4. Serve the pork over rice or with your favorite sides.

PORK

Slow Cooker Pork Roast with Vegetables

The pork is cooked to perfection with a blend of herbs and spices, while the vegetables make a tasty and healthy side dish.

Food Preparation: 10-15min | Cook Time: 6-8 hours | Yield: 2 servings

Ingredients:
- 1 lb pork roast
- 1 tbsp olive oil
- 1 tsp dried thyme
- 1 tsp dried rosemary
- 1 tsp garlic powder
- 1 tsp onion powder
- 1/2 tsp salt
- 1/4 tsp black pepper
- 2 carrots, peeled and sliced
- 2 potatoes, peeled and diced
- 1 onion, sliced
- 1 cup chicken broth

Instructions:
1. Rub the pork roast with the olive oil and then sprinkle with the thyme, rosemary, garlic powder, onion powder, salt, and pepper.
2. Place the carrots, potatoes, and onion in the bottom of the slow cooker and pour the chicken broth over the top.
3. Place the seasoned pork roast on top of the vegetables.
4. Cover the slow cooker and cook on low for 6-8 hours, or until the pork is tender and cooked through.
5. Once cooked, remove the pork from the slow cooker and let it rest for a few minutes before slicing.
6. Serve the sliced pork with the vegetables and some of the cooking liquid as a sauce.

Slow Cooker Moroccan Lamb Stew

LAMB

Lamb cooked in a spicy tomato-based sauce with chickpeas, vegetables, and Moroccan spices, served over couscous or rice.

Food Preparation: 15-20min | Cook Time: 4-8 hours | Yield: 2 servings

Ingredients:
- 1 lb lamb shoulder, cut into cubes
- 1 onion, diced
- 2 garlic cloves, minced
- 1 tsp ground cumin
- 1 tsp ground coriander
- 1/2 tsp ground cinnamon
- 1/2 tsp ground ginger
- 1/4 tsp cayenne pepper
- 1/4 tsp salt
- 1 can (14.5 oz) diced tomatoes
- 1 can (15 oz) chickpeas, drained and rinsed
- 1/2 cup chicken or vegetable broth
- 1/4 cup chopped fresh cilantro
- 1 tbsp lemon juice

Instructions:
1. In a slow cooker, combine lamb, onion, garlic, cumin, coriander, cinnamon, ginger, cayenne pepper, and salt. Stir well to coat the lamb.
2. Add diced tomatoes with their juices, chickpeas, and broth to the slow cooker.
3. Cover and cook on low for 6-8 hours, or on high for 3-4 hours, until the lamb is tender.
4. Stir in cilantro and lemon juice. Serve hot with rice or bread.

OTHER

Sausage and Bean Casserole

A hearty and filling meal with sausages, beans and vegetables. Serve with crusty bread.

Food Preparation: 15-20min | Cook Time: 4-8 hours | Yield: 2 servings

Ingredients:
- 6 sausages
- 1/2 onion, chopped
- 2 garlic cloves, minced
- 1 can of cannellini beans, drained and rinsed
- 1 can of chopped tomatoes
- 1 tsp dried thyme
- Salt and pepper, to taste
- 1 cup chicken or vegetable broth
- 1 tbsp cornstarch
- 2 tbsp water
- Fresh parsley, chopped, for serving (optional)

Instructions:
1. Heat a large skillet over medium-high heat. Add a little oil and brown the sausages on all sides, about 5-7 minutes. Transfer the sausages to the slow cooker.
2. Add the chopped onion and minced garlic to the skillet. Cook, stirring occasionally, until the vegetables are softened, about 5 minutes.
3. Add the cannellini beans, chopped tomatoes, dried thyme, salt, and pepper to the skillet. Stir everything together and pour the mixture over the sausages in the slow cooker.
4. Pour the chicken or vegetable broth into the slow cooker and stir everything together.
5. Cover the slow cooker and cook on low for 6-8 hours or on high for 3-4 hours.
6. In the last 30 minutes of cooking, mix the cornstarch and water in a small bowl to make a slurry. Pour the slurry into the slow cooker and stir everything together. Cook for an additional 30 minutes, until the sauce has thickened.
7. Serve the sausage and bean casserole with chopped fresh parsley, if desired.

Printed in Great Britain
by Amazon